Micros are fun

written by TONY GRAY Cert Ed, M A
Director of the Loughborough Primary Micro Project,
Loughborough University of Technology

and

CARL BILLSON Cert Ed, M A, M Sc
Loughborough Primary Micro Project,
Loughborough University of Technology

Ladybird Books Loughborough

Playing with words

Your micro is like a magic typewriter. Words can appear and vanish, change colour, chase each other over a page and do lots of tricks. The television screen is the 'paper' and writing is positioned on the screen page just as we position ships in the game of battleships.

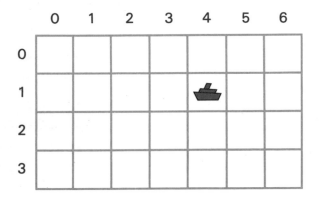

This ship is at row 1, column 4 or (1,4). Or it could be at (4,1) depending on whether you put the row or column first. (Spectrum and BBC computers differ in this! Look in your manual.)

Imagine an invisible grid, like the one below, on your computer screen. Letters, figures and graphics characters printed by your computer are positioned within this imaginary grid, just like the ship.

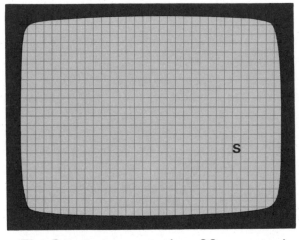

The Spectrum screen has 22 rows and 32 columns. To get the letter 'S' in this position on your screen, type:

> PRINT AT 15,27;"S"

The BBC micro, in MODE 7, has a screen with 32 rows and 40 columns. To get the letter 'B' in this position on your screen, type:

> PRINT TAB (5,25);"B"

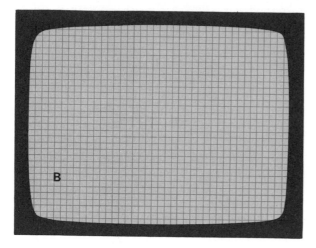

(In other modes the size of the grid varies. See your *BBC User Guide*.)

Try printing your name in each corner of the screen and in the middle.

WHAT'S NEXT?

Do you know what twenty policemen would say?

NO!

HELLO! HELLO! HELLO!

Try this :

```
10 FOR N = 1 TO 20
20 PRINT "Hello! Hello! Hello!"
30 NEXT N
```

These words will appear very quickly. How could you make a pause between each row of writing? (Look at the program on page 5 called *Walk*.)

3

The following program makes a picture of a wall from the word BRICK. Notice that the picture builds up from the bottom. How could you make this happen?

```
 20 CLS
 30 INK 2
 40 FOR y=20 TO 1 STEP -2
 50 FOR x=1 TO 25 STEP 5
 60 PRINT AT y,x;"BRICK"
 70 PRINT AT y-1,x+2;"BRICK"
 80 FOR W=1 TO 40: NEXT W
 90 NEXT x
100 NEXT y
110 INK 3
120 PRINT AT 10,7;"          "
130 PRINT AT 11,6;"  This is a
    "
140 PRINT AT 12,8;"    HOLE!  "
150 PRINT AT 13,10;"
    "
160 INK 0
```

```
 20 CLS
 30 REM uses colour in background and
 40 REM a procedure
 50 brickcol=129
 60 FOR row = 22 TO 1 STEP -2
 70 FOR brickpos = 3 TO 30 STEP 6
 80 PRINT TAB(brickpos,row)CHR$(brickc
ol)"BRICK"
 90 PRINT TAB(brickpos+3,row-1)CHR$(br
ickcol)"BRICK"
100 FOR delay = 1 TO 500 : NEXT delay
110 NEXT brickpos
120 NEXT row
130 PROChole
140 END
150 REM ******************************
160 DEF PROChole
170 PRINT TAB(10,10)"     "TAB(20,10)
"      "TAB(11,11)"
"TAB(13,12)CHR$131" This is a "TAB(12,1
3)"    "CHR$131"HOLE!    "TAB(11,14)"

180 ENDPROC
```

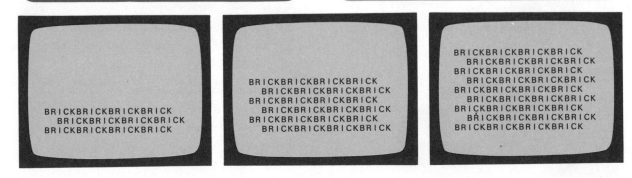

4

HOW CAN I GET MOVING WORDS?

Easy! Have you ever used a flick book? Each picture is slightly different from the one before so that when you flick through them quickly, your eye sees steady movement. Cartoons and all film animation work like this.

Try taking a word for a walk!

```
10 FOR N=1 TO 20
20 PRINT AT 10,N;"WALK"
30 PAUSE 25
40 NEXT N
```

```
10 FOR N=1 TO 20
20 PRINT TAB(N,10)"WALK"
30 FOR J=1 TO 250:NEXT
40 NEXT N
```

There is a trail of Ws that needs to be rubbed out. Change line 20 by putting a blank space in front of WALK so that it now looks like this:

" WALK"

This works! The extra space 'covers' the letter W each time.

What effect would you get with:
".WALK"

Now that you're getting words to move, why not stage a race — say between HARE and TORTOISE?

Other commands can change the colour of the writing, make some words flash or change the background colour. Try including some of these effects in your programs. Your computer manual will have details.

See if you can use the word CROSS several times to make the shape of a cross, or SQUARE, repeated and arranged as a square. Can you think of other words which suggest their own shapes?

Making pictures

How about making pictures with a computer? Computer pictures are called GRAPHICS and nearly all computers can make them.

Well, let's think about how pictures are made. Find a newspaper and take a close look at one of the photographs. Can you see that it's made from lots of dots? Use a magnifying glass to see them better.

Computer graphics are also made out of dots which are actually little squares, called *pixels*, arranged in rows and columns. The more squares you have, the clearer the image.

OK. What about a triangle?

Using squares, the more we have the better the triangle.

The problem is that you have to work in rows and columns on a computer. On a snooker table for example, at the beginning of a game; the reds make a triangle but they're not in rows and columns.

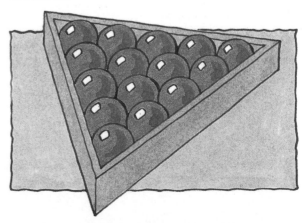

If you use a lot of squares on a computer screen, you can create a really good triangle in rows and columns. Notice that the edges don't look as jagged.

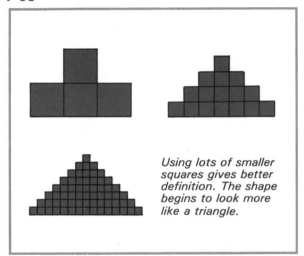

Using lots of smaller squares gives better definition. The shape begins to look more like a triangle.

This could be used to make a road sign for example.

If there are only a few big squares on the screen, the pictures are called LOW-RESOLUTION graphics. If there are a lot of small squares, we have HIGH-RESOLUTION graphics.

Let's draw a space invader. First you'll need to work out where the squares should go. Use some squared paper.

1 Draw your space invader on paper. Here's mine...

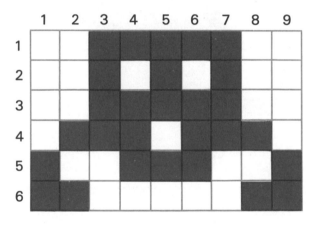

2 Check your computer manual to find the code which makes the machine print a square. On the Spectrum it is code 143; on the BBC micro it is code 255. On both these machines, code 32 makes a blank space.

Make another invader, putting numbers in for squares and spaces.

Here's mine...

32	32	143	143	143	143	143	32	32
32	32	143	32	143	32	143	32	32
32	32	143	143	143	143	143	32	32
32	143	143	143	32	143	143	143	32
143	32	32	143	143	143	32	32	143
143	143	32	32	32	32	32	143	143

4 We then use a short program to instruct the computer to draw our invader. You can write your own if you wish (Hint: use a READ statement in a loop), or there's a program below to draw my invader. Just type in your own DATA instead of mine. If your invader is a different size change lines 20 and 30 (BBC lines 20 and 40.) When you run the program, it will draw your invader!

3 Now we need to give these to the computer. We can do this by using DATA statements...

```
1000 DATA 32,32,143,143,143,143,143,32,32
1010 DATA 32,32,143,32,143,32,143,32,32
1020 DATA 32,32,143,143,143,143,143,32,32
1030 DATA 32,143,143,143,32,143,143,143,32
1040 DATA 143,32,32,143,143,143,32,32,143
1050 DATA 143,143,32,32,32,32,32,143,143
```

```
10 CLS
20 FOR y=1 TO 6
30 FOR x=1 TO 9
40 READ char
50 PRINT CHR$ char;
60 NEXT x
70 PRINT
80 NEXT y
100 DATA 32,32,143,143,143,143,
143,32,32
110 DATA 32,32,143,32,143,32,14
3,32,32
120 DATA 32,32,143,143,143,143,
143,32,32
130 DATA 32,143,143,143,32,143,
143,143,32
140 DATA 143,32,32,143,143,143,
32,32,143
150 DATA 143,143,32,32,32,32,32
,143,143
```

```
10 CLS
20 FOR Y=1 TO 6
30 PRINTCHR$151;
40 FOR X=1 TO 9
50 READ char
60 PRINT CHR$(char);
70 NEXT
80 PRINT
90 NEXT
100 DATA 32,32,255,255,255,255,255,32,
32
110 DATA 32,32,255,32,255,32,255,32,32
120 DATA 32,32,255,255,255,255,255,32,
32
130 DATA 32,255,255,255,32,255,255,255
,32
140 DATA 255,32,32,255,255,255,32,32,2
55
150 DATA 255,255,32,32,32,32,32,255,25
5
```

Have a look at the projects on pages 20, 24 and 28. They use a similar method to make different pictures.

Super sounds

To make sounds, the computer needs information about how long each note lasts (*duration*) and whether it is a high or low sound (*pitch*). Each computer has its own commands to make sounds, so have a look in your manual.

Here are some sounds. Try them...

```
BEEP 5,25
BEEP 1,-30
BEEP .1,0
```

```
SOUND 3,-15,201,100
SOUND 3,-15,29,20
SOUND 3,-15,101,2
```

Change the values and listen to the effects.

Here's a little program which will play changing sounds. Can you see how it works?

```
10 FOR I=1 TO 3
15 REM J goes up
20 FOR J=10 TO 20
30 BEEP 0.1,J
40 NEXT J
45 REM K goes down
50 FOR K=-10 TO -20 STEP -1
60 BEEP 0.1,K
70 NEXT K
75 REM now repeat
80 NEXT I
```

```
10 FOR scale=1 TO 10
20 FOR pitch=0 TO 255 STEP 15
30 SOUND 3,-15,pitch,3
40 NEXT pitch
50 NEXT scale
```
Try changing line 30 to:
30 SOUND 0,-15,pitch,3

The way to finding interesting sounds is to play about with the values and see what happens. You could change any of the numbers in the program lines above and alter the sound.

Another thing to remember is that sounds are best included in a program for a special reason. This reason will then help you to decide about the sound.

For example you might want to have a warning sound to go with the *Hands Off!* message on page 32. If you look at the *Happy Birthday* project (page 16) you will find that the tune is important.

So when you think about a sound, ask...

> *Does it need to be long or short?*
> *Will it be high or low?*
> *Should it be musical or just a noise?*
> *Is it there to draw attention*
>   *to something?*
> *Is the sound regular and repeating?*
> *Does it have to fit a rhythm?*

What kind of sound would fit a Christmas card?

What about the sound of a red alert?

What noise would a space invader make?

GO ON!
MAKE A NOISE
—NOW!

Computer projects

On the following pages there are some projects for you to try.

They're not just for you to copy but are ideas to start you off on your own programs. Don't forget that you can use the information in the first part of the book to help you. To make your programs interesting try using sound, pictures, colour, movement and words.

Don't forget to plan your program. All programmers plan their projects very carefully. This is called *designing* the program.

They often use squared paper to help them to get the pictures and words in the right place before they start writing the program in BASIC (Beginner's All Symbol Instruction Code.) They also use *flow charts* to make sure that things happen in the right order. Here's one. Can you follow it?

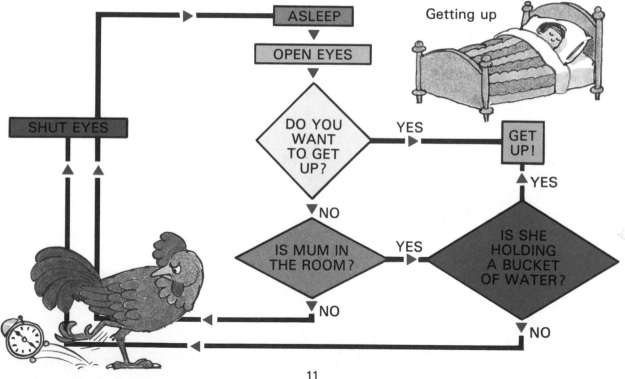

Getting up

ASLEEP
↓
OPEN EYES
↓
DO YOU WANT TO GET UP? — YES → GET UP!
↓ NO   ↑ YES
IS MUM IN THE ROOM? — YES → IS SHE HOLDING A BUCKET OF WATER?
↓ NO   ↓ NO
SHUT EYES

Project 1

Crack-a-joke

You can make the computer tell jokes!

Who wrote the book *Programming small machines*?

Think of your jokes and then arrange the program so that you can tell a lot of jokes one after another like a joke book! You press a key to carry on. (See *Super writer* on page 32 for a hint on how to do this.)

Some different kinds of jokes are Knock! Knock! jokes.

Do you know these:

MIKE O'COMPUTER

Mother: What's that Concorde doing in your bedroom?

Son: I must've left the landing light on!

Knock knock who's there?
Howard
     Howard who?
Howard I know

Why did the banana go out with the prune?

He couldn't find a date!

12

Here's a jokes program to get you started.

```
 20 DIM f$(5,10)
 30 DIM p$(5,30)
 40 FOR i=1 TO 5
 50 READ f$(i),p$(i)
 60 NEXT i
 70 CLS
 75 LET j=INT (RND*5)+1: INK 0
 80 PRINT AT 3,6;"Knock! Knock!
"
 90 PAUSE 0
100 PRINT AT 5,6;"Who's there?"
110 PAUSE 50
120 PRINT AT 7,8;f$(j)
130 PAUSE 0
140 PRINT AT 9,8;f$(j);" who?"
150 PAUSE 50
160 CLS : INK 2
170 PRINT AT 10,1;p$(j)
180 PAUSE 0
190 GO TO 70
200 DATA "    Albert","Albertel
lin' you later!"
210 DATA "    Walter","Walter t
errible joke!"
220 DATA "      Will","Will you
 let me in!!!!"
230 DATA "    Doctor","How did
you know?"
240 DATA " Superman.","Why? How
 many others are there?"
```

```
 20 REM Reads jokes into arrays for 1st
 30 REM and second parts
 40 DIM firstline$(5),pun$(5)
 50 FOR I = 1 TO 5
 60 READ firstline$(I),pun$(I)
 65 NEXT I
 70 CLS
 80 joke=RND(5)
 90 PRINTTAB(10,10) "Knock! Knock!"
100 ch$=GET$
110 PRINTTAB(10,12) "Who's there?"
120 FOR I = 1 TO 1500 : NEXT I
130 PRINTTAB(10,14)firstline$(joke)
140 ch$=GET$
150 PRINTTAB(10,16)firstline$(joke)" w
ho?"
160 FOR I = 1 TO 1500 : NEXT I
170 CLS
180 PRINTTAB(2,12)CHR$141pun$(joke)
190 PRINTTAB(2,13)CHR$141pun$(joke)
200 ch$=GET$
210 GOTO 70
220 DATA "Albert","Albertellin' you la
ter!"
230 DATA "Walter","Walter terrible jok
e!"
240 DATA "Will","Will you let me in!!"
250 DATA "Doctor.","How did you know?"
260 DATA "Superman.","Why? How many ot
hers are there?"
```

Project 2
Kaleidoscope

In a kaleidoscope, mirrors are arranged so that one pattern is reflected and repeated to make several patterns.

We can do a similar thing on a computer and make the patterns keep changing. You could also add sounds.

Have you ever made an ink blot picture like this?

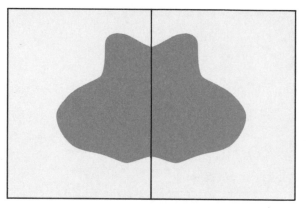

Notice that the pattern is in two halves and it looks as though there is a mirror in between. We call this a *symmetrical* pattern.

Let's start with a simple pattern.

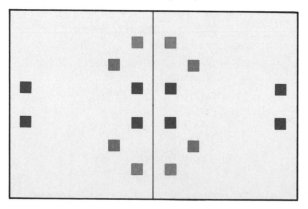

To do this on a computer you print something in one half of the screen and tell the computer to work out where the 'reflection' will be.

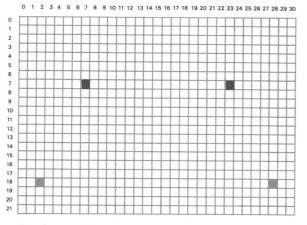

Let's see how we work out the position of the reflected blocks. The red block is in column 7 in the left half of the screen. Its reflection is in column 23. This position is 7 places in from the last column which is 30. The blue block fits the same pattern. It's in column 2 and its reflection is in column 30-2.

To get lots of blocks we can use the command RND to make the computer select different positions.

Try to write a program that will create a kaleidoscope pattern like the one opposite.

Then try dividing your screen into four sections and print blocks in the top left-hand section which are reflected in the other three sections.

```
20 LET d=INT (RND*20)
30 LET a=INT (RND*15)
40 LET i=1+INT (RND*7)
50 INK i: PRINT AT d,a;"█"
60 PAUSE 10
70 INK i: PRINT AT d,31-a;"█"
80 PAUSE 10
90 GO TO 20
```

```
10 CLS
20 xpos=RND(18)
30 ypos=RND(23)
40 PRINT TAB(xpos,ypos)CHR$(255)
50 PRINT TAB(38-xpos,ypos)CHR$(255)
60 FOR I=1 TO 500:NEXT
70 GOTO 20
```

Project 3

Happy Birthday

Why not design and send a personal video greetings card? It might be for a birthday, Christmas, a Valentine, Mother's day, Congratulations or Easter. This 'card' could draw itself, play a tune and send a message all in one! You can use ideas from other sections of this book (eg *Sounds* & *Super writer*) so don't forget to look through the rest of the book.

To get the tune, look in your computer manual for the values to put in the BEEP or SOUND command for each note. The names of the notes are the letters above the music. You may have to experiment to get the correct *duration* or length of sound.

```
20 LET d=.5
30 LET p=12
40 BEEP d/2,p+2: BEEP d/2,p+2:
BEEP d,p+4: BEEP d,p+2: BEEP d,
p+7: BEEP d*2,p+6
50 BEEP d/2,p+2: BEEP d/2,p+2:
BEEP d,p+4: BEEP d,p+2: BEEP d,
p+9: BEEP d*2,p+7
60 BEEP d/2,p+2: BEEP d/2,p+2:
BEEP d,p+14: BEEP d,p+11: BEEP
d,p+7: BEEP d,p+6: BEEP d,p+4
70 BEEP d/2,p+12: BEEP d/2,p+1
2: BEEP d,p+11: BEEP d,p+7: BEEP
d,p+9: BEEP d*2,p+7
```

```
20 FOR N=1 TO 25
30 READ pitch,duration
40 SOUND 1,-15,pitch,duration
50 X=INKEY(30)
60 IF N=7 THEN X=INKEY(130)
70 IF N=13 THEN X=INKEY(130)
75 IF N=20 THEN X=INKEY(100)
90 NEXT
100 END
110 DATA 109,5, 109,5, 117,10, 109,10,
129,10, 125,20
120 DATA 109,5, 109,5, 117,10, 109,10,
137,10, 129,20
130 DATA 109,5, 109,5, 157,10, 145,10,
129,10, 125,10, 117,10
140 DATA 149,5, 149,5, 145,10, 129,10,
137,10, 129,20
```

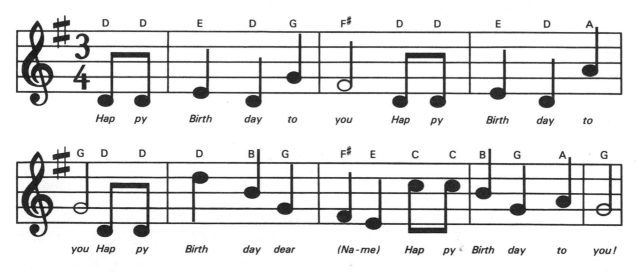

Project 4
Brain box

How about a quiz to test your friends? It could be about anything you like – as long as you know the answers! You could try questions about your hobbies, pop music, sports, famous people, record breakers – anything!

To do this the computer has to know the questions and be able to match them to the answers. Here are two ways of setting a quiz...

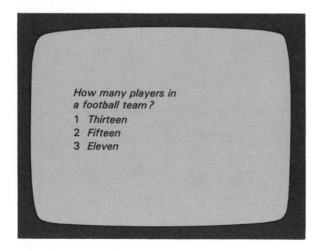

*How many players in
a football team?*
1 *Thirteen*
2 *Fifteen*
3 *Eleven*

Here the computer knows that the correct answer is number 3 and if you type in the numeral it gives you a message, such as, 'Correct', and gives you a point.

In this one the computer will only say, 'Correct' if the person types in the correct answer which, in this example, would be Rome.

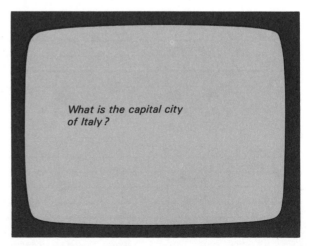

*What is the capital city
of Italy?*

Here's a small program to start you off:

```
10 FOR I=1 TO 2
20 INK 0: CLS
30 READ q$,a$
40 PRINT : PRINT : PRINT q$
50 PRINT : PRINT : INPUT r$
60 IF r$=a$ THEN PRINT : PRINT
: INK 1: PRINT "Correct!!": GO
TO 90
70 PRINT : PRINT "No, try agai
n."
80 GO TO 50
90 FOR J=1 TO 500: NEXT J
100 NEXT I
110 DATA "What is the capital o
f France?","PARIS"
120 DATA "Which country is Madr
id in?","SPAIN"
```

```
 5 FOR I = 1 TO 2
10 CLS
20 READ question$,answer1$,answer2$
30 PRINT'''question$
40 INPUT''reply$
50 IF reply$ = answer1$ OR reply$=ans
wer2$ THEN PRINT''CHR$(130)"Correct!!":G
OTO90
60 PRINT'''"No, try again."
70 GOTO40
90 FOR J=1 TO 2000:NEXT
95 NEXT I
100 DATA"What is the capital of France
?","Paris","PARIS"
110 DATA"What country is Warsaw in?","
Poland","POLAND"
```

This little program doesn't set out the questions very well, it doesn't keep score, it doesn't accept small letters as the answer and it doesn't ask questions which have a choice of answers. Can you make your program do these things?

19

Project 5
Galactic guide

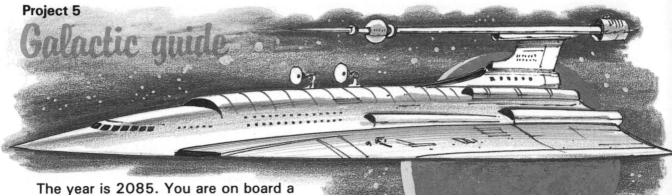

The year is 2085. You are on board a Star Cruiser speeding across the expanse of space. The mission is to explore planet XEPTON 3 in the ROGA PLANAR solar system.

So far the voyage has been routine, with the on-board computer controlling navigation. But the deeper you go into space, the more you need to rely on your Galactic Guide.

This important manual is an electronic book. At the press of a button you can call up information. The Galactic Guide has entries about most of the things you're likely to need: which planets have suitable living conditions; hostile or friendly alien life forms; food and drink; enemy spacecraft and holiday planets.

Why not choose a section, eg vehicles, and design video 'pages' for the Guide?

You could have several entries in each section. To get from one page to another you press the SPACE BAR or some other key. (Look at the *Super writer* program on page 32: Spectrum line 30, BBC line 100 shows a way of doing this.)

The section you choose need not be about spacecraft. It could be about fantastic beasts and unusual creatures, food and drink around the galaxy or good entertainment places to visit while journeying across solar systems.

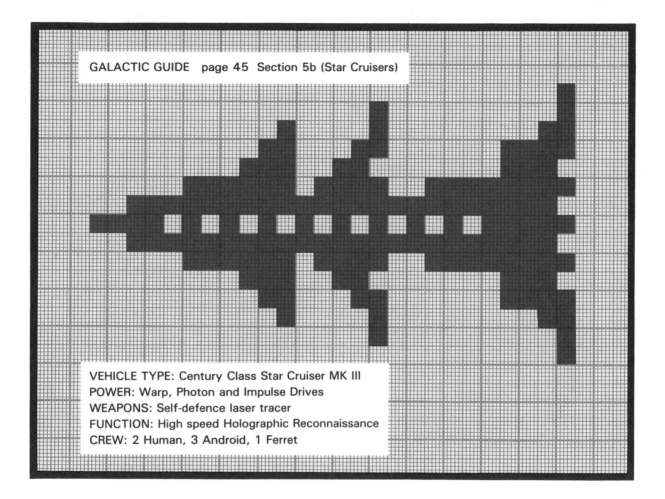

GALACTIC GUIDE   page 45 Section 5b (Star Cruisers)

VEHICLE TYPE: Century Class Star Cruiser MK III
POWER: Warp, Photon and Impulse Drives
WEAPONS: Self-defence laser tracer
FUNCTION: High speed Holographic Reconnaissance
CREW: 2 Human, 3 Android, 1 Ferret

Of course, you could make a spotter's guide book about anything, not just space. For example: sports, pets, pop groups, recipes, in fact whatever interests you! Each page of your computer guide could have a picture or some facts, or both.

Project 6
Flying

Many cartoon or animated films are created with the help of computers. On page 5 we looked at ways of moving words on the screen. Here we are making a cartoon bird fly!

Imagine you saw these three pictures one after the other quite quickly. 1,2,3 – 1,2,3 – 1,2,3...and so on.

This is what we need to do on the computer to get our flying bird.

It's like using drawings in flick books to get moving pictures.

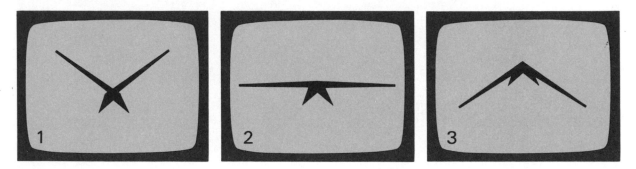

Each picture is made by PRINTing the shape. For example, picture 1 is done like this:

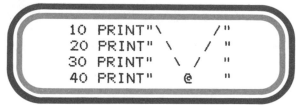

```
10 PRINT"\      /"
20 PRINT" \    / "
30 PRINT"  \  /  "
40 PRINT"    @    "
```

You could type this in and run it if you like.

(In MODE 7 on the BBC machine a \ will be printed as a ½ in your program listing, so use another mode, say MODE 4. On the Spectrum the \ sign is below letter D.)

Now we can design our program to make the bird fly:

1 Show picture 1, pause and clear the screen.
2 Show picture 2, pause and clear the screen.

22

3 Show picture 3, pause and clear the screen.
4 Repeat as many times as you like.

Have a go at making your own flying bird. Below is a short program to compare with your own.

```
 10 LET X=0
 20 CLS
 30 PRINT AT 6,X;"\     /"
 40 PRINT TAB (X);"  \   /"
 50 PRINT TAB (X);"   \ /"
 60 PRINT TAB (X);"    @"
 70 PAUSE 3: CLS
 80 PRINT AT 9,X;"---@---"
 84 PAUSE 3: CLS
 88 PRINT AT 9,X;"   @"
 90 PRINT TAB (X);"   / \"
100 PRINT TAB (X);"  /   \"
110 PRINT TAB (X);"/     \"
120 PAUSE 1.5: CLS
130 LET X=X+1: IF X>25 THEN LET
X=0
140 GO TO 30
```

```
 30 X=0
 40 CLS:PRINT'''''
 50 PRINTTAB(X)"\     /"
 60 PRINTTAB(X)"  \   /"
 70 PRINTTAB(X)"   \ /"
 80 PRINTTAB(X)"    @"
 90 FORW=1TO400:NEXT:CLS:PRINT'''''
100 PRINT'''TAB(X)"---@---"
110 FORW=1TO400:NEXT:CLS:PRINT'''''
120 PRINT'''TAB(X)"    @"
130 PRINTTAB(X)"   / \"
140 PRINTTAB(X)"  /   \"
150 PRINTTAB(X)"/     \"
160 FORW=1TO200:NEXT:CLS:PRINT'''''
170 X=X+1:IFX>30 THEN X=0
180 GOTO40
```

There are lots of ways of using animation in programs. Imagine starting an adventure program with a magic dragon on the wing! Other ideas you might try are a see-saw, a pendulum on a grandfather clock or a catherine wheel firework.

Project 7

Take a chance!

Here's taking a chance with a difference: games that use dice will never seem the same once you start using screen dice!

Whatever the game you are playing: Snakes and Ladders, Monopoly or Dungeons and Dragons, your next move may be decided by the roll of a dice.

Computers have a command – RND – that allows us to pick numbers in a random way. Let's use your computer to roll dice on the screen.

On pages 7 and 8 we made a space invader. Design your dice in the same way, like this:

Plan your program so that a number from 1 to 6 is picked at random. Let's say a 5 is chosen. Instead of printing a figure 5, the computer prints your dice design.

In the program below the dice appear in different positions on the screen so that it looks as if they really have rolled around. Not only that, the dice are coloured too! But you never know which colour will be rolled next.

```
  10 CLS
  20 REM dice
  30 col$=CHR$(RND(7)+144)
  40 x=RND(35):y=RND(18)
  50 PRINT TAB(x-1,y)col$"ppppp"
  60 FOR Y=y+1TO y+4
  70   PRINT TAB(x-1,Y)col$;
  80   FOR X=x TO x+4
  90     PRINT TAB(X,Y) CHR$255;
 100     NEXT
 110   PRINT
 120   NEXT
 130 ON RND(6) GOSUB1000,2000,3000,4000
,5000,6000
 140 CH$=GET$:GOTO 10
1000 VDU31,x+2,y+2,96:RETURN
2000 VDU31,x+1,y+1,96,31,x+3,y+3,96:RET
URN
3000 VDU31,x+1,y+1,96,31,x+2,y+2,96,31,
x+3,y+3,96:RETURN
4000 VDU31,x+1,y+1,96,31,x+3,y+1,96
4010 VDU31,x+1,y+3,96,31,x+3,y+3,96
4020 RETURN
5000 GOSUB4000:GOSUB1000:RETURN
6000 GOSUB4000:VDU31,x+1,y+2,96,31,x+3,
y+2,96:RETURN
```

```
15 PAPER 0: INK 7: CLS            510 PRINT AT d+1,a;"▙▙▙"
20 LET i=1+INT (RND*7)            520 PRINT AT d+2,a;"▛▛▙"
25 INK i                          530 PRINT AT d+3,a;"▙▙▙"
30 LET N=1+INT (RND*6)            540 RETURN
35 LET a=1+INT (RND*26)           600 PRINT AT d,a;"▁▁▁"
38 LET d=INT (RND*17)             610 PRINT AT d+1,a;"▙▙▙"
40 IF N=1 THEN GO SUB 100         620 PRINT AT d+2,a;"▛▛▛"
50 IF N=2 THEN GO SUB 200         630 PRINT AT d+3,a;"▙▙▙"
60 IF N=3 THEN GO SUB 300         640 RETURN
70 IF N=4 THEN GO SUB 400
75 IF N=5 THEN GO SUB 500
80 IF N=6 THEN GO SUB 600
90 PAUSE 0: GO TO 20
100 PRINT AT d,a;"▁▁▁"
110 PRINT AT d+1,a;"▛▛ "
120 PRINT AT d+2,a;"▛▛ "
130 PRINT AT d+3,a;"▛▛ "
140 RETURN
200 PRINT AT d,a;"▁▁▁"
210 PRINT AT d+1,a;"▛▛▛"
220 PRINT AT d+2,a;"▛▛ "
230 PRINT AT d+3,a;"▛▛▛"
240 RETURN
300 PRINT AT d,a;"▁▁▁"
310 PRINT AT d+1,a;"▛▛▛"
320 PRINT AT d+2,a;"▛▛▛"
330 PRINT AT d+3,a;"▛▛▛"
340 RETURN
400 PRINT AT d,a;"▁▁▁"
410 PRINT AT d+1,a;"▙▙▛"
420 PRINT AT d+2,a;"▛▛ "
430 PRINT AT d+3,a;"▙▙▛"
440 RETURN
500 PRINT AT d,a;"▁▁▁"
```

That could make games interesting. Imagine playing Snakes and Ladders. Each player chooses a colour. When the dice appear on the screen you can only use the score shown if it's in your colour! Dice games will never be the same!

As Dungeons and Dragons players will know, some games need different kinds of dice. You can have 8, 12, 20-sided dice – any number you like using the computer. The design is up to you. Pictures, words or numbers can all make interesting dice. Why stop at just one?

Project 8

Star signs

Capricorn ♑

Aquarius ♒   Pisces ♓   Aries ♈

Star Sign	Ends on Day
Capricorn	20
Aquarius	50
Pisces	79
Aries	110
Taurus	140
Gemini	171
Cancer	201
Leo	232
Virgo	265
Libra	295
Scorpio	326
Sagittarius	356

Some magazines use slightly different dates to those above. Alter your program if you wish to change them.

Capricorn, Taurus, Leo and Libra are some of the Signs of the Zodiac. What's your star sign? Most people read their stars in the newspapers for fun. Some people believe that the astrologer's predictions can come true.

This program will work out a person's star sign. You type in a birth date and the computer tells you which Sign of the Zodiac it comes under. You could then add to the program by having the computer give the person's fortune.

We want the computer to 'read' a birth date, eg 14.02.72, and to calculate from this how many days that is into the year. If January 1st is *day 1* of the year, February 14th will be *day 45* (31 + 14). Next the computer must compare the day number with its stored list which defines the Signs of the Zodiac like this:

February 14th, or *day 45*, is less than *day 50* (45<=50), so it falls under the Star Sign Aquarius.

See if you can design a program that will work out star signs. The following program may help to start you off.

Notice that it will need finishing. Not all the star signs are there and line 230 (line 300 on the BBC) is only included so that the program will run as it is written.

26

```
  20 INPUT "Please type in your
date of     birth. e.g. 09.03.72
 ";b$
  30 LET d =VAL (b$( TO 2))
  40 LET m =VAL (b$(4 TO 5))
  50 IF m=1 THEN LET s=d
  60 IF m=2 THEN LET s=d+31
  70 IF m=3 THEN LET s=d+59
  80 IF m=4 THEN LET s=d+90
  90 IF m=5 THEN LET s=d+120
 100 IF m=6 THEN LET s=d+151
 110 IF m=7 THEN LET s=d+181
 120 IF m=8 THEN LET s=d+212
 130 IF m=9 THEN LET s=d+243
 140 IF m=10 THEN LET s=d+273
 150 IF m=11 THEN LET s=d+304
 160 IF m=12 THEN LET s=d+334
 170 IF s>356 OR s<21 THEN LET s
$="Capricorn": GO TO 310
 180 IF s<51 THEN LET s$="Aquari
us": GO TO 310
 190 IF s<80 THEN LET s$="Pisces
": GO TO 310
 200 IF s<111 THEN LET s$="Aries
": GO TO 310
 210 IF s<141 THEN LET s$="Tauru
s": GO TO 310
 220 IF s<172 THEN LET s$="Gemin
i": GO TO 310
 230 LET s$="not in        my dat
a"
 310 INK 2
 320 PRINT "Your birth sign is "
;s$;"."
 330 PAUSE 600: CLS : GO TO 10
```

```
  10 MODE7
  20 INPUT''''"Please type your date of
birth         (e.g. 28.09.71) "bday$
  30 d=VAL(LEFT$(bday$,2))
  40 m=VAL(MID$(bday$,4,2))
  50 IF m=1 THEN s=d
  60 IF m=2 THEN s=d+31
  70 IF m=3 THEN s=d+59
  80 IF m=4 THEN s=d+90
 .90 IF m=5 THEN s=d+120
 100 IF m=6 THEN s=d+151
 110 IF m=7 THEN s=d+181
 115 IF m=8 THEN s=d+212
 120 IF m=9 THEN s=d+243
 130 IF m=10 THEN s=d+273
 140 IF m=11 THEN s=d+304
 160 IFm=12 THEN s=d+334
 180 IF s>=357 OR s<=20 THEN s$="Capric
orn":GOTO310
 190 IF s<=50 THEN s$="Aquarius":GOTO31
0
 200 IF s<=79 THEN s$="Pisces":GOTO310
 210 IF s<=110 THEN s$="Aries":GOTO310
 220 IF s<=140 THEN s$="Taurus":GOTO310
 230 IF s<=171 THEN s$="Gemini":GOTO310
 300 s$="not in my data"
 310 PRINT '''CHR$141CHR$129"Your star
sign is "s$"."

 400 CH=GET:GOTO10
```

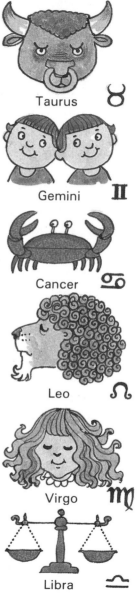

Taurus ♉

Gemini ♊

Cancer ♋

Leo ♌

Virgo ♍

Libra ♎

27

Your program could be one that told fortunes for fun. It could have many predictions stored in memory which are picked at random to resemble an astrologer's forecast. (See items using RND in this book or the section *Stories, Jokes and Poems*, page 3 in the Ladybird computer book *Projects for Programs*.)

Other ideas:

1 Make your program more personal by asking for and using the person's name.
2 Design a picture for each Sign of the Zodiac.
3 Get your predictions to unfold slowly and with great mystery, perhaps from a crystal ball. See the program for *Talking Heads* on the next page.

Scorpio   ♏

Sagittarius   ♐

Project 9

Talking heads

HELLO I'M SPIKE!

Computers can do things very very quickly. For example, they can print whole pages on a screen almost before you have time to blink. Even a line of writing (text) appears all at once.

People read more slowly than computers print, just as, when we listen to someone, it takes time for us to hear the whole message.

Sometimes it is useful to have messages appear slowly on the computer screen. It could be a secret message unfolding before your eyes, a joke, a prediction or someone talking.

This simple program will start you off.

```
 20 CLS
 30 PRINT : PRINT : PRINT
 40 PRINT " !!!!!!!!!!!"
 50 PRINT " *         *"
 60 PRINT "_* (.)(.) *_"
 70 PRINT "\*        */"
 80 PRINT " *   /\   *"
 90 PRINT " *        *"
100 PRINT " *        *"
110 PRINT " * \__/   *"
120 PRINT " *        *"
130 PRINT " ****  ****"
140 PRINT "    *  *"
150 PRINT "    *  *"
160 PRINT "*****  *****"
170 PRINT LET r=1+INT (RND*2)
180 IF r=1 THEN LET A$="Hi ther
e!"
190 IF r=2 THEN LET A$="Pleased
to meet you."
200 FOR f=1 TO LEN A$
210 PRINT AT 11,f+11;A$(f)
220 PAUSE 10
230 NEXT f
```

```
 20 MODE4
 30 PRINT'''" !!!!!!!!!!!!"
 40 PRINT" *         *"
 50 PRINT"_* () () *_"
 60 PRINT"\*        */"
 70 PRINT" *   /\   *"
 80 PRINT" *        *"
100 PRINT" *        *"
110 PRINT" *        *"
120 PRINT" *****  *****"
130 PRINT"    *  *"
140 PRINT"    *  *"
150 PRINT"*****  *****"
160 IF RND(2)=1 text$="Hi there!!!!" E
LSE text$="Pleased to meet you."
170 FOR I = 1 TO LEN(text$)
180 PRINT TAB(19+I,11) MID$(text$,I,1)
;
190 FOR J = 1 TO 500::NEXT
200 NEXT
210 PRINTTAB(0,20)
```

Project 10

Tongue twister test

How quickly can you say this?

She sells seashells on the seashore.

It's quite hard isn't it!

The computer could time you to see whether you get better with practice. It could also give you a new tongue twister to try.

It works like this...

1 The computer says, 'Get Ready.'
2 The timer starts. The tongue twister appears and you have to say it correctly.
   (No cheating!!)
3 Press a key as soon as you have said it.
4 The computer prints your time on the screen.

This is quite easy to program. Here's a simple version.

```
10 CLS
20 PRINT AT 3,5;"How quickly c
an you say a";AT 4,8;"ting twist
er?"
30 PAUSE 100
40 CLS
50 LET delay=INT (RND*50)+100
60 READ t$
70 IF t$="All done." THEN CLS
: STOP
80 PAUSE delay
90 CLS : BEEP .5,10: PRINT AT
10,0;t$
100 LET j=0
110 LET j=j+1: IF INKEY$="" THE
N GO TO 110
120 PRINT AT 14,10;j/125;" seco
nds"
130 PAUSE 150
140 GO TO 30
150 DATA "She sells sea shells
on the sea shore."
160 DATA "Red lorry, yellow lor
ry."
170 DATA "All done"
```

```
   10 CLS
   20 PRINT TAB(7,9)"How quickly can you
say"TAB(11,13)"a tingue twoster?"
   30 FOR I = 1 TO 5000:NEXT
   40 CLS
   50 pause =  RND(400)+200
   60 VDU7:PRINTTAB(16,11)"READY"
   70 READ twister$
   80 IF twister$="All done" THEN CLS:EN
D
   90 FOR I = 1 TO pause*10:NEXT
  100 CLS:VDU7:PRINT''''''''twister$
  110 TIME=0
  120 ch$=GET$
  130 PRINT''''''TIME/100 " seconds"
  140 ch$=GET$
  150 GOTO 40
  160 DATA She sells sea shells on the s
ea shore.
  170 DATA"Red lorry, yellow lorry"
  180 DATA"All done"
```

To improve this you could have a title page, extra tongue twisters, print the name of the fastest person and their time, make a comment on the time (eg 'That's not very fast!'), or make the tongue twisters gradually harder.

Timing things in this way is useful in all kinds of programs, especially quizzes and games.

Here are some more tongue twisters.

> *Red lorry, yellow lorry*
> *Sheep shouldn't sleep in a shack, sheep should sleep in a shed*
> *A noisy noise annoys an oyster!*
> *Peter Piper picked a peck of pickled pepper.*

Can you make up some others?

Project 11
Super writer!

The ordinary letters on a computer are small. What about being able to put big letters on the screen? These could be used in program titles, posters, surprises, warnings, making words stand out and sending letters to a superhero!

Remember how we did an invader on pages 7 and 8? You can use the same method to make your big messages.

What about writing a trick program so that if someone presses a key on the computer while you are away, a big message like 'HANDS OFF!' flashes on the screen and a warning siren sounds?

```
10 CLS : INK 0
20 PRINT AT 20,0;"© SINCLAIR R
esearch 1982"
30 LET C$=INKEY$: IF C$="" THE
N GO TO 30
40 IF C$="?" THEN GO TO 80
50 CLS : FLASH 1
60 PRINT AT 10,10;"HANDS OFF!"
70 BEEP 5,20
80 INK 0: FLASH 0
```

```
 90 PRINT")";
100 ch$=GET$
110 IF ch$="?" THEN GOTO 160
120 CLS
130 PRINT TAB(12,13)CHR$(141)"HANDS OF
F!!"
140 PRINT TAB(12,14)CHR$(141)"HANDS OF
F!!"
150 SOUND 0,-15,1,100
160 REM continue program from here
```